I Am the Moon

REBECCA AND JAMES MCDONALD

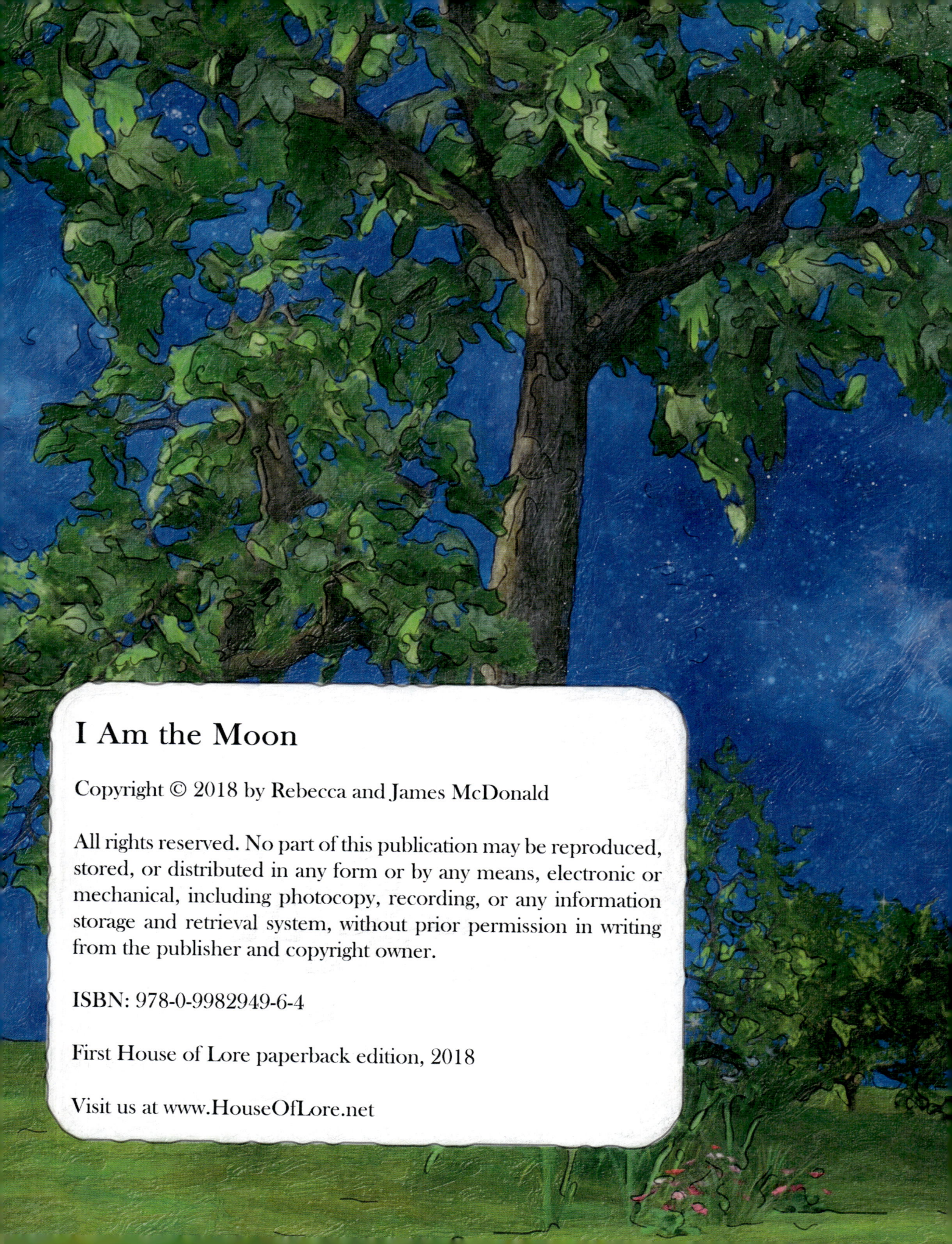

I Am the Moon

Copyright © 2018 by Rebecca and James McDonald

All rights reserved. No part of this publication may be reproduced, stored, or distributed in any form or by any means, electronic or mechanical, including photocopy, recording, or any information storage and retrieval system, without prior permission in writing from the publisher and copyright owner.

ISBN: 978-0-9982949-6-4

First House of Lore paperback edition, 2018

Visit us at www.HouseOfLore.net

Don't worry! You can see all the creatures again and build another sandcastle during the next low tide, when I pull the water away from the beach again.

When the Sun shines bright on me, I get really hot, and when the Sun goes down, it gets really cold, so astronauts must wear spacesuits to protect themselves.

That means lifting a car or an elephant is easier. But make sure the elephant brings a space helmet to wear.

If astronauts visiting my surface accidently drop something, like their lunch or a favorite toy, they'll have plenty of time to catch it before it hits the ground. Weak gravity makes things fall more slowly.

Here are some things you can do to become an astronaut and visit the Moon:

1. Work hard in school.
2. Work extra hard at math and science.
3. Read a lot of books about space and the Moon.
4. Eat healthy and exercise to build a strong body.
5. Write to the National Aeronautics and Space Administration (NASA), and ask the scientists who work there what you can do to prepare to be an astronaut. Right now, NASA is the number one employer of astronauts in America.

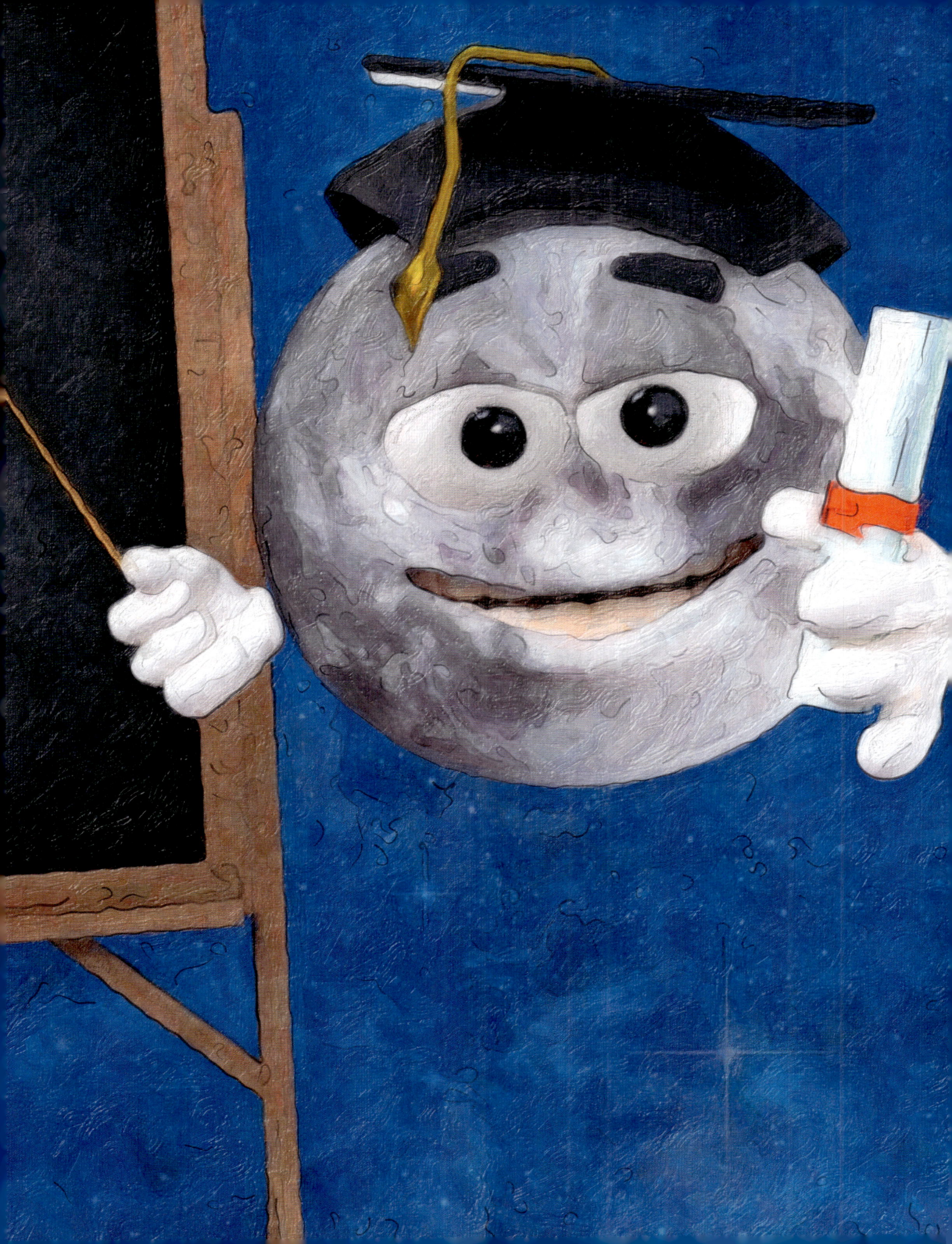

Made in the USA
Middletown, DE
27 November 2021